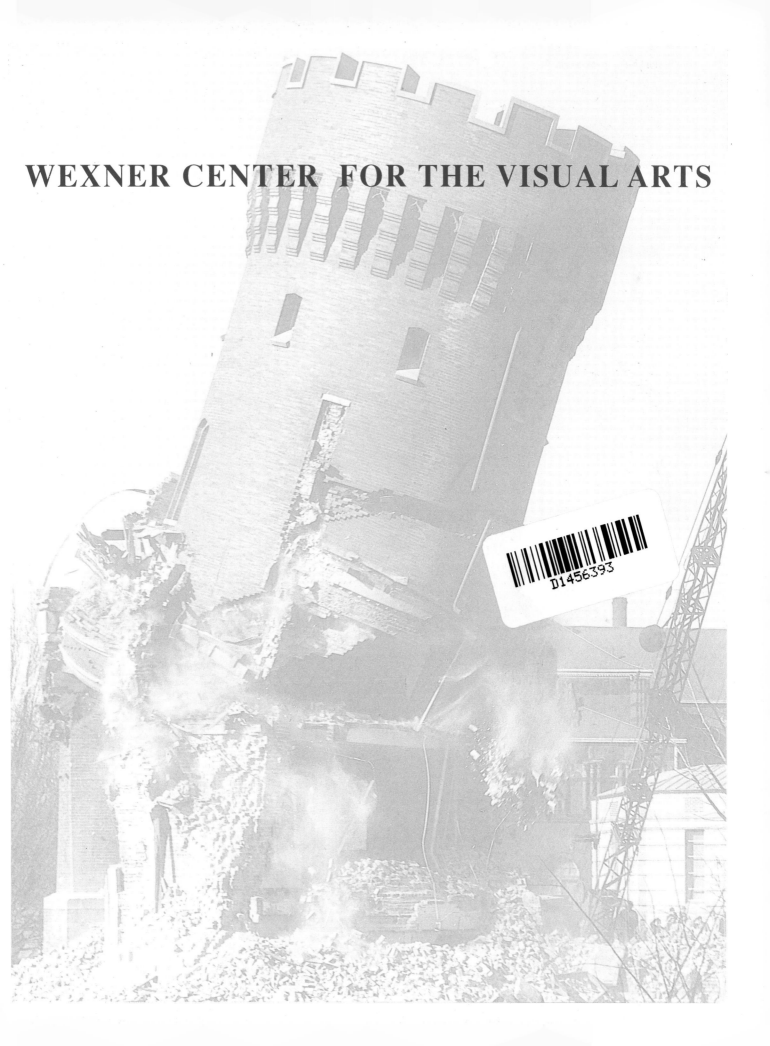

WEXNER CENTER FOR THE VISUAL ARTS

D1456393

An Architectural Design Profile

ACADEMY EDITIONS · LONDON / ST. MARTIN'S PRESS · NEW YORK

Acknowledgements

Client The Ohio State University, Columbus, Ohio *University Architect:* Richard Eschilman *University Project Architect:* James Swiatek *University Project Manager:* Tom Heretta. **Architect** Eisenman/Trott Architects, Inc, New York and Columbus, Ohio *Partners-in-Charge:* Peter Eisenman, Richard Trott *Directing Architects:* Michael Burkey, George Kewin *Project Architects:* Arthur Baker, Andrew Buchsbaum, Thomas Leeser, Richard Morris, James Rudy, Faruk Yorgancioglu *Project Team:* Andrea Brown, Edward Carroll, Robert Choeff, David Clark, Chuck Crawford, Tim Decker, Ellen Dunham, Frances Hsu, Wes Jones, Jim Linke, Michael McInturf, Hiroshi Maruyama, Mark Mascheroni, Alexis Moser, Harry Ours, Joe Rosa, Scott Sickeler, Madison Spencer, Mark Wamble. **Consultants** *Landscape Architects:* Hanna/Olin, Ltd, Philadelphia; *Partner-in-Charge:* Laurie Olin *Structural Engineer:* Lantz, Jones & Nebraska, Inc *Partner-in-Charge:* Tom Jones *Mechanical Engineer:* H A Williams & Associates *Lighting Design:* Jules Fisher & Paul Morantz, Inc., *Civil Engineer:* C F Bird & P J Bull, Ltd *Security and Fire:* Joseph M Chapman, Inc *Graphics and Colour:* Robert Slutzky *Soils Engineer:* Dunbar Geotechnical *Audio Visual:* Boyce Nemec *Specifications:* George Van Neil *Models:* Albert Maloof, Gen Servini, Scale Images *Renderings:* Brian Burr *Model Photography:* Dick Frank, Wolfgang Hoyt *Construction Photographs:* James Friedman, Will Shively and D G Olshavsky/ARTOG *Final Photographs:* Jeff Goldberg/ESTO and D G Olshavsky/ARTOG. **Contractors** *General Contractor:* Dugan and Meyers *Project Manager:* Jim Smith *Mechanical Contractor:* A T F Mechanical, Inc *Project Manager:* Rob Weiland *Electrical Contractor:* Romanoff Electric *Project Superintendent:* Sib Goelz *Plumbing Contractor:* Radico, Inc *Project Manager:* Frank Czako *Steel Subcontractor:* J T Edwards *President:* Jack Edwards

Editor: Dr Andreas C Papadakis First published in Great Britain in 1989 by *Architectural Design* an imprint of the ACADEMY GROUP LTD, 7 HOLLAND STREET, LONDON W8 4NA ISBN: 1-85490-0277 (UK) Copyright © 1989 the Academy Group. *All rights reserved* The entire contents of this publication are copyright and cannot be reproduced in any manner whatsoever without written permission from the publishers. The Publishers and Editor do not hold themselves responsible for the options expressed by the writers of articles or letters in this magazine. Copyright of articles and illustrations may belong to individual writers or artists *Architectural Design* Profile 82 is published as part of *Architectural Design* 59 : 11-12 : 89 Published in the United States of America by ST MARTIN'S PRESS, 175 FIFTH AVENUE, NEW YORK 10010 ISBN: 0-312-04471-2 (USA) Printed and bound in Singapore

Contents

A PERSONAL NOTE
PHILIP JOHNSON

During the competition, I was against the Eisenman project because I thought it did such violence to both the programme and the campus; I was absolutely wrong. The Wexner is a terrific success against all odds. Not only would his solution never have crossed my mind, but after seeing his design at the project stage, even then I never would have imagined it possible that it would succeed. I did not think that one could create a grand space by wrecking two adjacent buildings and jamming an axis between them.

During the competition I was for Graves' scheme. At that time, I was very sympathetic with his attitude, his intention to design a building in which pictures could hang with some dignity and cultural reference. All of my training, all of my understanding of what produces a fine architecture, all of my interest in classical architectural themes – in wanting to know where I was in relationship to place, in wanting to know where I entered, in wanting to know where the pictures would be and how they would be celebrated – all of these considerations led me to Micheal's scheme. Though these themes exist in the Wexner building, they are rendered virtually irrelevant by an architectural expression of willful energy and sheer delight.

With Michael Graves' Portland Building, there was a real sense that it marked a change in architecture. The Wexner is also marking a turning point in American architecture, though in a much more profound way. I think that postmodernism was a reaction – an important one – but merely a reaction nonetheless. The Wexner, on the other hand, portends a more fundamental change of architecture. From the beginning, Portland was easy to understand in terms of the design and it's cultural motives. The Wexner on the other hand is a very mysterious building, one which requires an almost entirely new set of perceptions. It does not rely on familiar patterns of architectural thinking and it is not legible in the terms which we are conditioned to expect. It fits neither with the modernism of Meier nor the nostalgia of Micheal Graves; it is not a product of the cult of pretty drawings; it does not emerge from an appropriate relationship with it's surroundings.

What's different about the Wexner is that when you review these well-known criteria – modernist, postmodernist, contextualist and so forth, none apply. Yet at the same time the Wexner, borrows from each of them. There is a contextural attitude, but not simple contextualism. There is a postmodernist attitude, but not simple postmodernism. There is a modernist attitude, but not a simple modernism. Peter has taken elements which would usually be associated with other architectures, ones antagonistic to his own work, and used those elements against those architectures. For example, the armory quotation, which would be normally associated with postmodern, is fragmented and shifted, and thus used against the simple nostalgia for the place characteristic of postmodernism.

The armory in the Wexner is both a nostalgic image and a displacing image? It is the central part of the fragmentation system, which actually became more prominent during design development. I think it is just perfect. It speaks to a reminiscence for the region, while at the same time playfully opposing such nostalgia. Peter, I think, reminded American architecture that architecture could make you uncomfortable, that it was not necessarily dedicated to comfort or beauty. The axis which would normally be associated with a contextualism is likewise used against contextualism. So the building turns the strengths of the very architecture that Eisenman is concerned to oppose against those architectures. He has the courage to blast the baggage, the presuppositions that architects carry around in their minds. Depth courage, foolhardiness, idiocy, ignorance and brilliance all at once.

Peter was very lucky. He had a potent site sufficiently constrained to force his work. There was all the money in the world. The programme that was so elastic that it was almost unrestricted. Someday, someone might say of the Wexner, 'Let's clear out this junk that past generations have piled into here. We have got to celebrate this wonderful axis and we are not going to have it cluttered up with old-fashioned pictures on the wall'.

Eisenman had no idea while designing it that the Wexner would produce such experiential quality. Such accidents only happen to good architects. The Seagram Building was better than Mies could have imagined; it too was such an accident. Accidents of all sorts – in the design process, in the personality of the client, in the eventualities of construction – are essential to architecture. For example, a series of accidents, including an inefficient bureaucracy which abdicated close scrutiny, a generous patron, and so forth combined to give Eisenman a chance to express himself in the Wexner in a way he may never have again.

When a great architect stumbles upon enough means to be able to express themselves fully – including expressing their mistakes –architecture is always the ultimate beneficiary. There are serious errors in the Wexner, the lack of resolution at the north-end, for example. But the totality of it is a much, much greater success than any of us could have forseen. What is new in Eisenman, and what insures that his impact will be more than that of an idiosyncratic visionary is the fact that he has taken it upon himself to learn to negotiate to his projects.

You do not measure an architect by his bad buildings or even his average buildings, but by his great buildings. Wexner is a great building. Most of us would have thought to merely do a nice building. Peter Eisenman seized the opportunity to blast the entire architectural scene open. What courage. What ignorance.

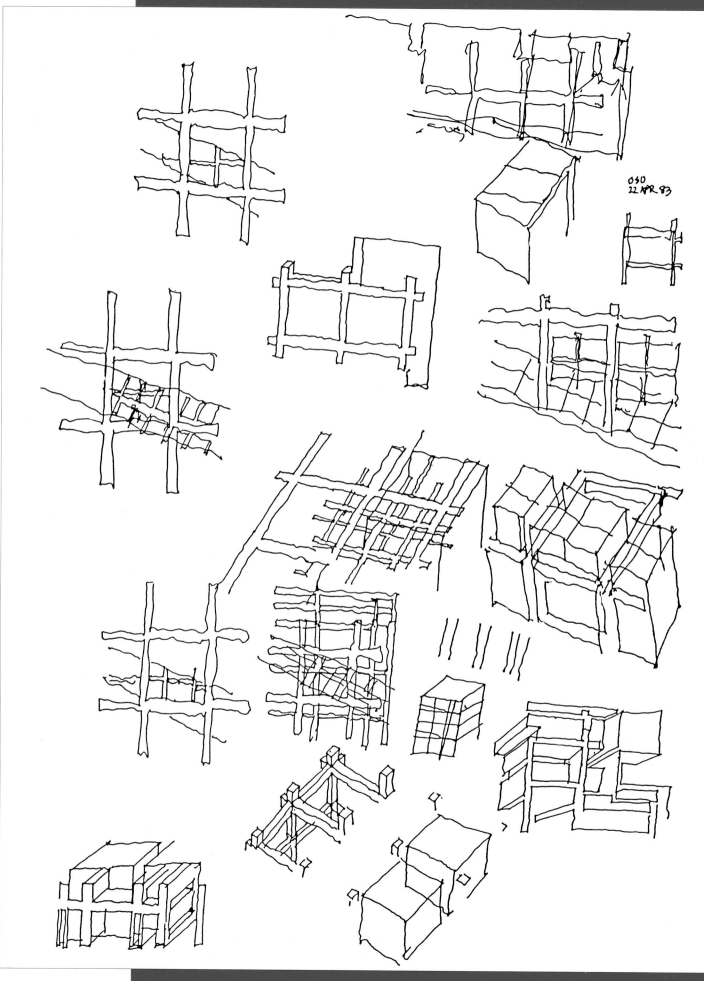

OSO
22 APR 83

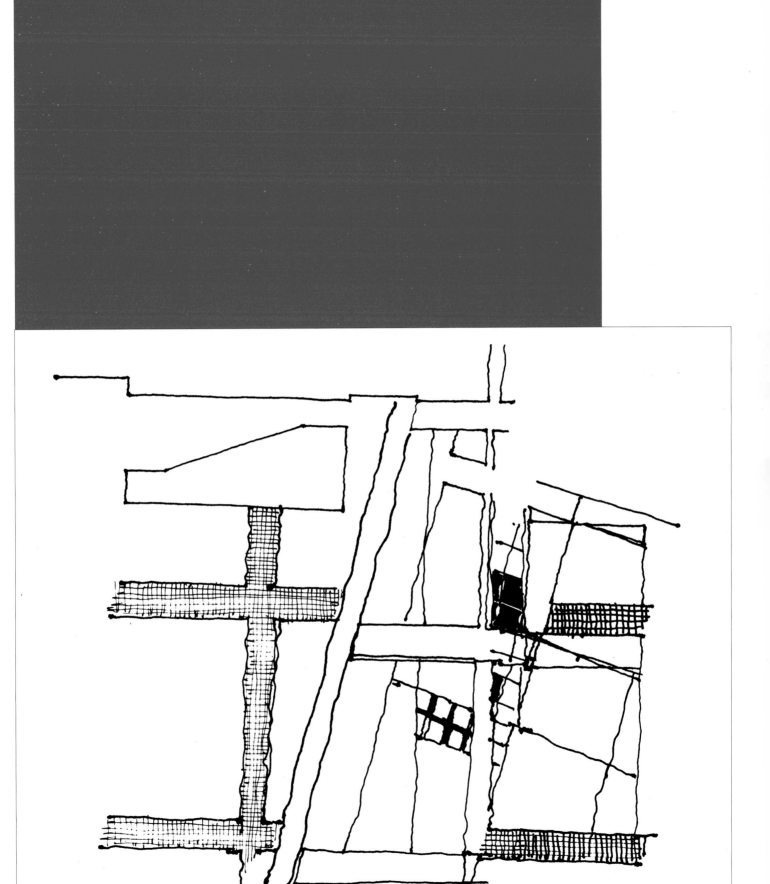

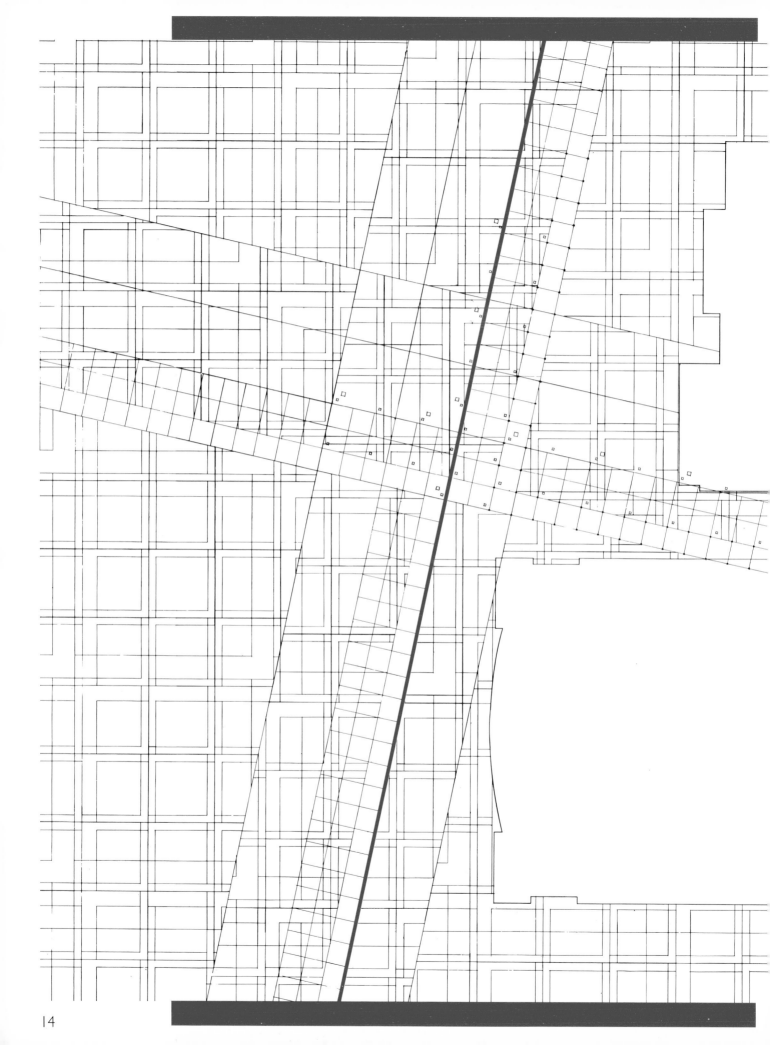

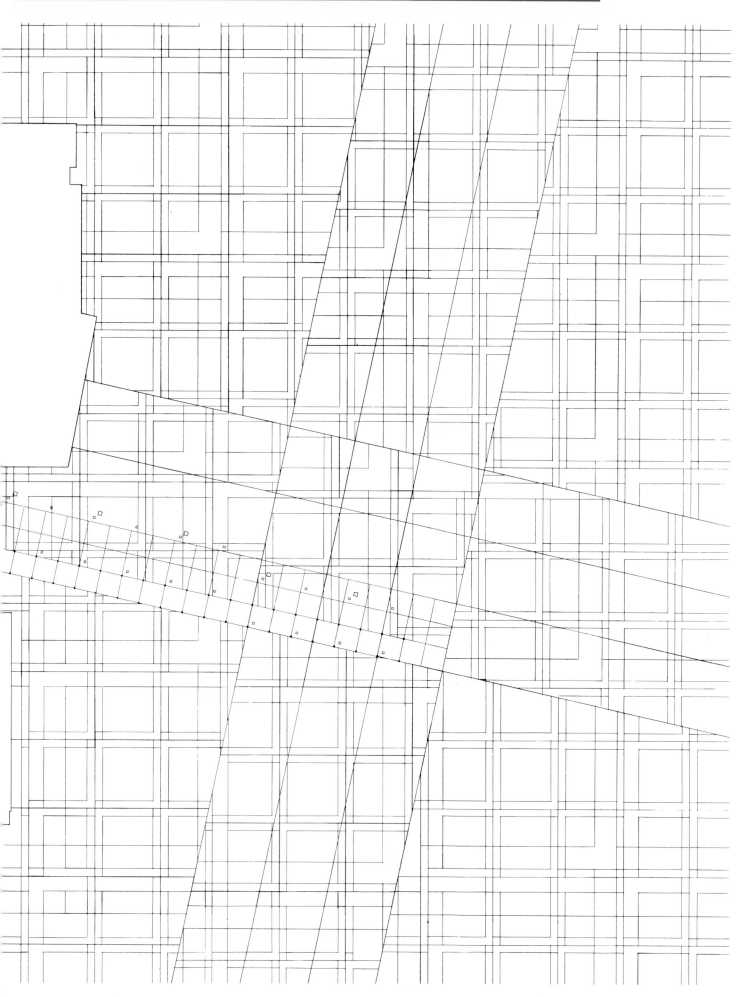

UPPER LOBBY

OPEN TO
OHIO GALLERY
BELOW

MERSHON AUDITORIUM

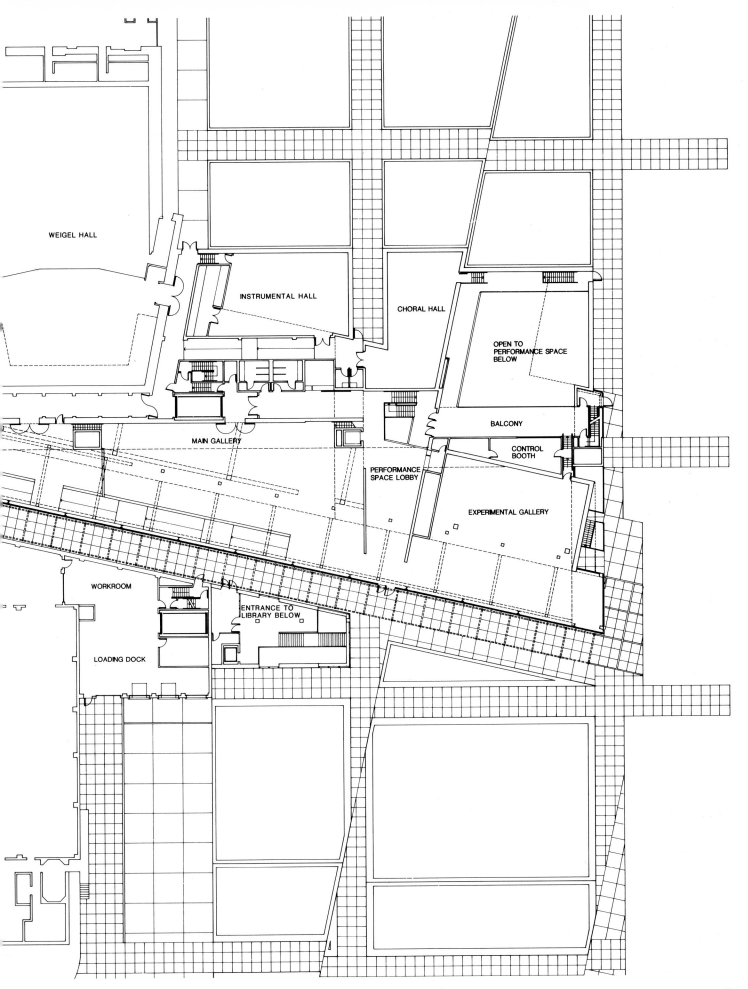

WEIGEL HALL

INSTRUMENTAL HALL

CHORAL HALL

OPEN TO
PERFORMANCE SPACE
BELOW

MAIN GALLERY

BALCONY

CONTROL
BOOTH

PERFORMANCE
SPACE LOBBY

EXPERIMENTAL GALLERY

WORKROOM

ENTRANCE TO
LIBRARY BELOW

LOADING DOCK

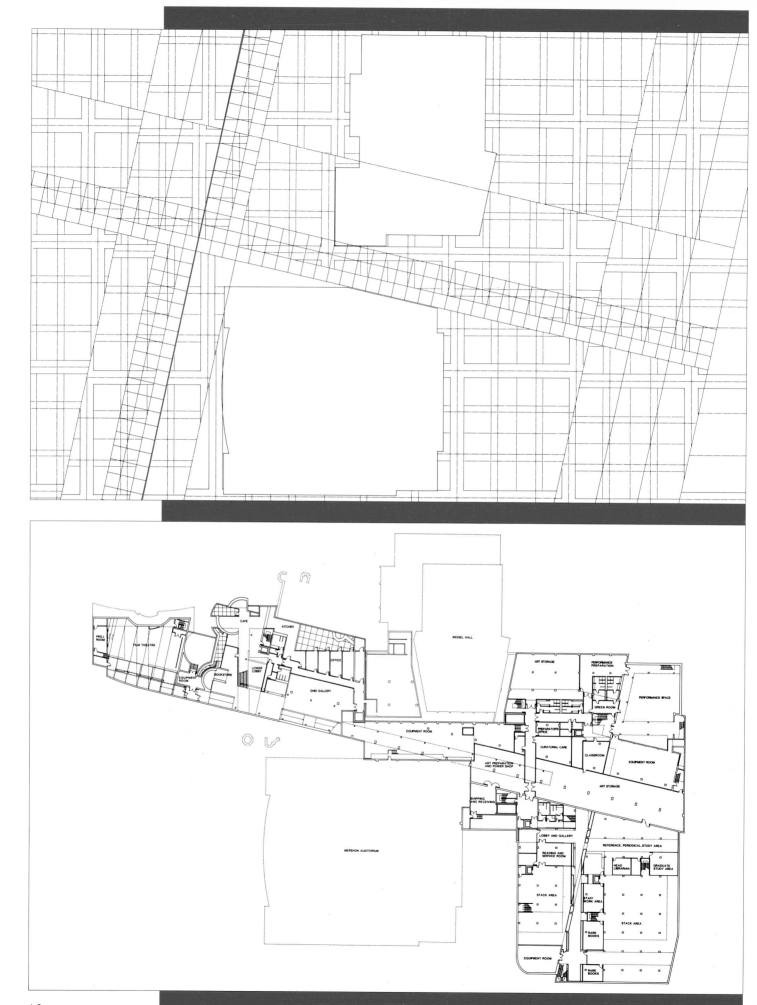

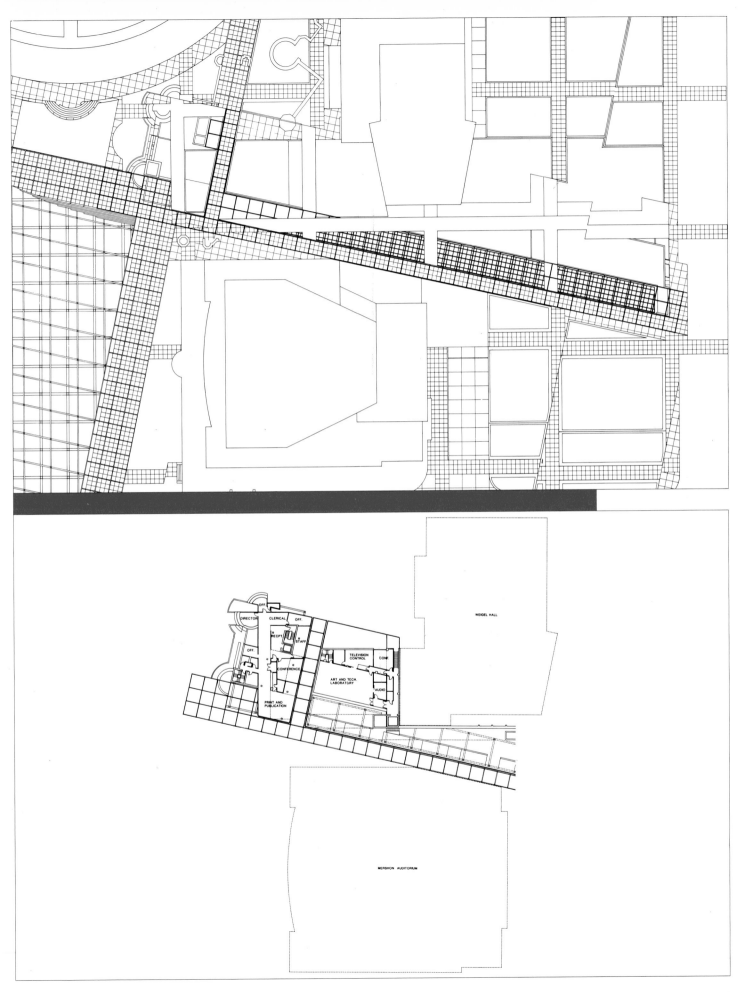

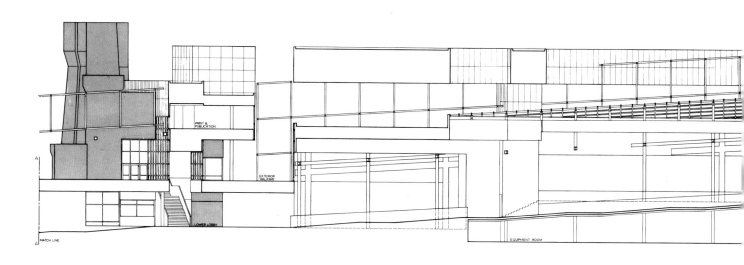

PRINT &
PUBLICATION

EXTERIOR
WALKWAY

LOWER LOBBY

EQUIPMENT ROOM

A
A MATCH LINE

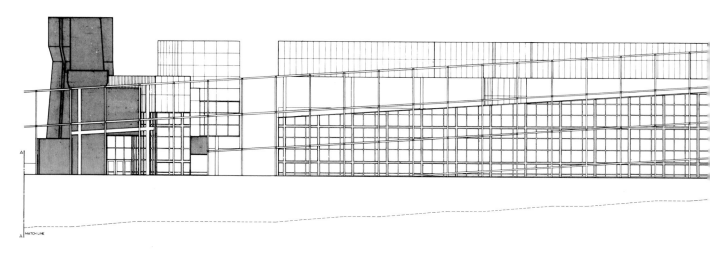

A
A MATCH LINE

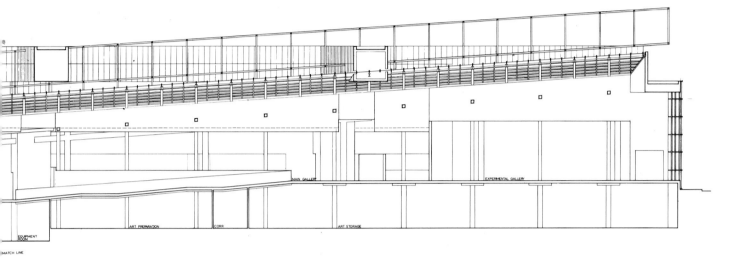

EQUIPMENT
ROOM

MATCH LINE

ART PREPARATION   CORR   ART STORAGE   MAIN GALLERY   EXPERIMENTAL GALLERY

B

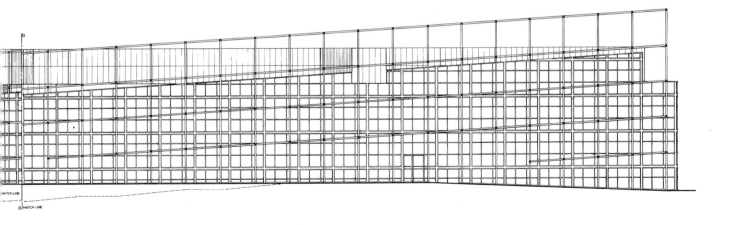

B

MATCH LINE

B MATCH LINE

EISENMAN'S WHITE HOLES
CHARLES JENCKS

Eisenman met my plane in Columbus Ohio at nine-thirty in the morning. I had been travelling for 24 hours – London, Boston, Los Angeles, Detroit, Columbus – which seemed like 24 days because of the space-time warp and no sleep. He was wearing a light jacket and trousers, his usual quizzical grin and a completely incongruous baseball cap with the letter C inscribed in the centre like the customary copyright sign – ©

Almost his first words were the kind of cross-examination one expects from this architectural logician. Inevitably the question focussed on the headgear perched on his greying cranium. 'Cincinnatti Reds?', I guessed, realising it was unlikely to be anything so obvious as a major league team that came from Ohio. No, this dislocated sign had another referent. 'Chicago Cubs?' No, we were not in Illinois – no logic there. I wondered, silently, why I had to go through this trial by conundrum before breakfast and whether there was not some special architectural significance to the C: perhaps a series of C-curves were embedded in his building? Yes, that was true, but not the answer. The cap simply came from the local farm club from Columbus, stupid – C – how could I miss the contextual trace since I was *in* the city and had actually flown *over* his building and its shifting grids – one oriented to the Columbus grid, one oriented to the campus grid. C-C, Columbus Clippers! You have to understand co-incidental paralogic!

Playing the Eisenman game
Eisenman loves non-sequitur logic, a baseball cap sitting on top of ivy league livery. It poses paradoxical questions like quantum physics with its ghost particles and complementary activities, its allowance for the sudden creation of matter out of energy. The only way you can understand quantum physics or almost any interesting cosmological point today is through the counter-intuitive logic of advanced mathematics. The only way you can decode an Eisenman building, or his simulacrum of such advanced sciences, is by asking him for an explanatory drawing and an *explication de texte*. Both are probably necessary for complete understanding – a point he might grant with the proviso of T.S. Eliot that architecture, like new poetry, is often most appreciated when only half-understood. Here there is a paradox, for Eisenman is caught between a desire to explain his ideas and make the building seem an inevitable consequence of their embodiment and; a contrary desire for obscurity and ambiguity. His notion of 'anti-memory' is a case in point, a kind of 'not-Post-Modernism' based on a series of 'nots'. As he wrote: 'We used the site as a palimpsest: a place to write, erase and re-write [history]. Our building reverses the process of the site inventing the building [Post-Modernism]. Our building invents the site [not-Post-Modernism].'

When we arrived at the building we were met by a site architect, and a PhD student at work on a thesis on Eisenman (or Venturi, he hadn't decided) and one of the most subtle explicators of Eisenman's work, Jeffrey Kipnis, a historian and critic. The five of us traversed the site and whenever Eisenman couldn't figure out the exact significance of a shifted grid, or a piece of polished granite, one of the other interpreters would supply the correct information. This reminded me of the ceremony which used to take place in a Chinese garden after it was built. Three or four poets and scholars would accompany the designer and complete the work by naming the parts, supplying an apt literary conceit here and historical reference there, and commenting on the beauty or lack of it. In our case this naming ceremony took place, but unfortunately we didn't subsequently mark the spots with inscriptions so future generations could gain from our deliberations and add their own. A good Chinese garden becomes a real palimpsest of successive comments and epigrams, a model which seems well suited to Eisenman's intentions of creating a labyrinthine architectural text.

As we entered the precinct we were met by the two basic grids – Columbus and campus – shifted at about $12\frac{1}{2}$ degrees to each other and picked out in the stone paths and two different types of tree. These led us at once in two directions – towards the main library towers straight ahead, and the Art Center's 'not-entrance' just to the right. This absent doorway is very visibly marked by the 'not-armory' to one side and the 'not-scaffolding' to the other. In fact the juxtaposition of these 'nots' is very picturesque and visually pleasing, a point of some anxiety to Eisenman who, when I pointed it out, intimated that he would rather be 'non-romantic and visual'. His game is first cerebral and second sensual and never, he hopes, just aesthetic. Just 'I like this balance' or 'move that shape over a bit', or 'let's tune the proportions somewhat'. He would never get involved in these games of taste and sensibility, refinement and whim. As a result the work, like Jim Stirling's, can appear somewhat wooden and awkward, the very opposite of I M Pei's facile primpings and tuckings.

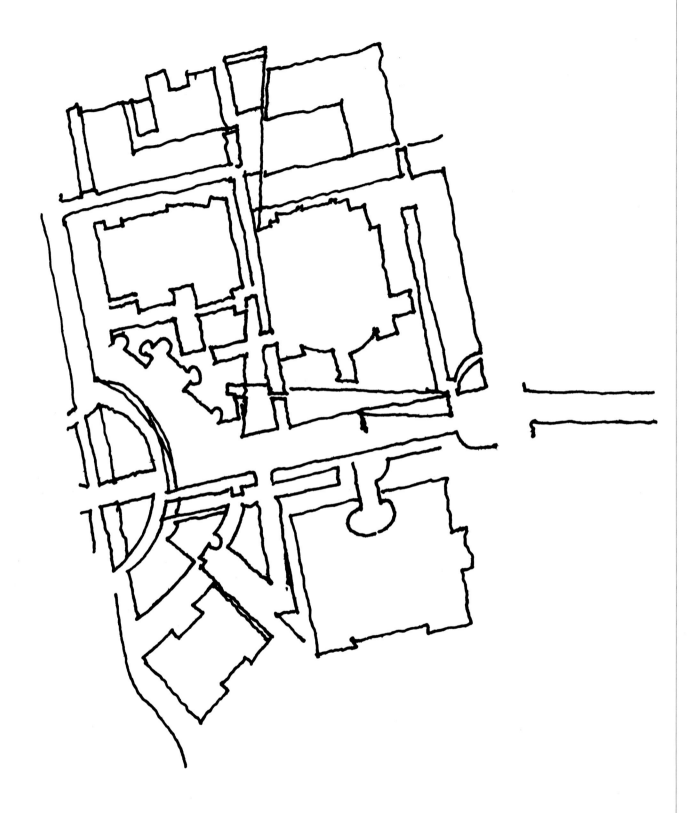

We traversed the 'not-doorway' and entered what will be the museum foyer when the building is finally finished. This has some wonderfully subtle juxtapositions of grids whose beauty will have to be fully appreciated later when the slight differences in greys and whites can be precisely gauged. Already this triple height space is a moving but not bombastic interplay of similar forms. The notion of 'scaling', which Eisenman has taken from fractal geometry and applied to grids, provides a continual visual interest – a kind of peaceful tension. All this sounds aesthetic, but it is really done for representational reasons. A sign of the organizing grids – different ones are represented at 12, 24, 48 and 96 feet – slices down through the roof and hangs ominously overhead – a 'not-column'. (In previous buildings Eisenman would leave out a column from his overall conceptual grid, but no-one except an informed critic would notice this 'absent presence': now it comes down from the ceiling for all to see its absence.) There are many other such structurally redundant signs, what could be called 'not-pilasters' since they have only a visual and conceptual role, but don't look like classical pilasters at all.

In fact they don't look like redundant markers either, and to make them fully understood Eisenman should have covered them with a particular colour or material as he has done, at least once, in the 'Black Box auditorium'. Then they wouldn't have been absorbed into the aesthetic experience of the real structural bay of 24 feet.

At any rate the foyer space and curving brick offices set up an effective counterpoint of figure and ground, representation and abstraction. The dark brick curves and turrets form a 'not-armory', a reminiscence of the 19th-century building that stood on part of the site. This was 'not-excavated' and 'not-rebuilt'; rather its foundations were unearthed and paved over in brick about 15 feet below ground level to become a literal sign of the former reality. And then a notional version of the old armoury was built – with slices, fragments, unfinished C-curves, and changes of brick colour. All these dislocations indicate its virtual or symbolic role as a 'not-armory'. This, in Eisenmanese, is also a 'dissimulation' of the past. It 'affirms the significance of a major lost landmark in the Ohio State Campus and refers the University to a piece of its own history'.

Some people may find this reference to an old armory rather banal, a recollection of pseudo military might that is best forgotten, but Eisenman pointed out that many such land grant colleges of the 19th century were centred around armouries and thus they had a symbolic function as state castles for education – bastions which proclaimed the newly domesticated land and emergent state.

This particular version was originally meant to be built of a 'not-brick' material, but in the event two real engineering bricks were used – dark brown and red – which have a kind of pedestrian hardness. This, coupled with the notional shapes and flares of the turrets, produces a 'ghost' building à la Venturi: that is a caricature of an outline which follows in general terms the original building. The problem with a ghost building in engineering brick is the problem of the 'built diagram' – the lack of sensual specificity. These are cerebral, not living, ghosts.

But if the fragmented 'not-armory', with its 'not-gateway' to the west, is visually inert, the opposite is true of the 'not-scaffolding'. This is a paradoxical and lively space, at once a walk through the building without entering it, a north arrow plunging upwards and downwards, and a white steel grid which gives Sol LeWitt-like perspectives. When I mentioned this artist's endless white grids, Eisenman dismissed the reference; perhaps suffering a bit of 'anti-memory' about a previous influence. In any case the tilting rows of white boxes within boxes zooming in perspective into the sky and ground becomes the most memorable image in the 'non-building'. They are Neo-Modernist versions of Bramante's perspectival grids – endless rather than closed, four-dimensional rather than oriented in one direction, light rather than heavy, and cerebral rather than haptic. 'Not-Renaissance perspectives', I suppose, producing Eisenmanian 'white holes' wherever you look down them – inducing you to move forward.

Indeed the 'scaffolding-walk', and parallel with it the main gallery promenade, are the most impressive spaces. They are 'strong images', not the 'weak images' he now seeks in his more ambiguous work. Images of grids seen through grids, grids tilted to each other, grids played at three scales, grids played in four colours (white, grey, silver, dark-grey) – grids on the floor, wall, ceiling and in every direction.

Eisenman is married to the grid, just as Le Corbusier was to light; in the latter's case this led to the response, from Madame le Corbusier, that 'all this light is driving me crazy'. One can imagine the occasional thought of the future curator of the Wexner Center for Art of the 21st century: 'all those grids are driving the paintings crazy'. This is a response Eisenman has anticipated – even provoked with his beautiful, buzzing cages and glass walls filled with parallelopipeds. He seeks to 'recontextualize art', get it off the walls, off the easels, out of the frames, away from the pedestals; he seeks to 'attack it with architecture'. In his words 'Wexner tries to break down architecture as a frame for painting. It talks about art as an event – like computer art, performance art, art of the 21st century'. When

I pointed out that his buzzing grids might cast shadows over the art, and the glass walls cause glare, he answered that if this was not right for some art, paintings in frames, it could be sent down the street to the Columbus Museum. A very Neo-Modernist response.

Repressing traditional and conventional art is not always in Eisenman's character and in fact he has supplied an abundance of background wall space in some parts; so it will take a little sorting on the curator's part to separate that art which should be 'recontextualized' from that which should just hang about being itself. The point for Eisenman, who is a little tired of arrogant artists regarding architecture as a neutral background for their foreground, is that the building is the equal of art. In fact when it opens in November it will *be* the art for the next three months and – aside from the occasional John Cage or performance piece – just display itself. In February 1990 art works (miraculously of the 21st century) will be installed. But for a while viewers will walk through these grids, tilts and excavations playing the Eisenman game of catch the reference, dig the meaning, decode the paradox.

There are several propositions Eisenman has mentioned or written about, which might be kept in mind while viewing this 'not-art-building', otherwise one may miss, or misunderstand, an abstraction:

1   The two grids, shifted at $12\frac{1}{2}$ degrees, blast through an existing auditorium and hall to either side. They slice off parts, but then use the same stone material to rebuild parts of the new Wexner Center.
2   This repetition of the destroyed corners is 'simulation'.
3   The ghost building of the armoury, which no-one could mistake for the original, is 'dissimulation'.
4   The 'non-building' has neither beginning nor end, up nor down; it dissolves into the campus and landscape. In fact it treats the landscape as 'not-building', burrowing library underneath the ground.
5   These gridded mounds to east and west recall, for Eisenman, Indian mounds that are not far away in Ohio.
6   A slice, or cut, or tilted sheer in these mounds recalls, for Eisenman, the 'Greenville Trace' – that line of colliding grids which runs through Ohio. This collision was caused by using Thomas Jefferson's gridded plan for democratic America plus two conflicting measuring devices for magnetic north.
7   The 'not-scaffolding' represents an unfinished building awaiting its art of the future.
8   The tilted outdoor 'not-auditorium', with its skewed 'not-seats', visually turns the campus axis towards the Wexner Center. The larger curve of the adjacent road is taken up elsewhere in the 'not-building', especially in the curved wall of the interior auditorium.
9   The White Tower fast-food restaurant – on the road in from the airport – is not only an inspiration for Richard Meier's white enamelled panels of the last 15 years, but an influence on Eisenman's ghosted turrets in the 'not-armory'.
10 Eisenman and Meier are 'not-first cousins', but more distantly related.

This list of propositions and co-incidences is not complete, but it gives one a start in playing the Eisenman game, and from it many further correct and incorrect moves can be made. Eisenman won this building in a competition against his friends such as Michael Graves by siting his building exactly where no-one else would . . . correct. This building is radically different from Richard Meier's abstractions . . . incorrect.

The building is an elaborate chess game, or hermetic text to be unscrambled, or open-ended symbolic machine, and I'm sure Vincent Scully and a host of academic interpreters and icon-detectives will be kept busy for the next few years unpacking its clues. As Leo Tolstoy argued: Modern Art takes a large class of qualified professionals to decode its cryptic subtleties and critics, as a restless army, must be kept in employment or else they are bound to cause trouble. Eisenman is the best thing that has happened to the PhD industry since James Joyce.

On Not Playing the Eisenman game

Being a member of this inflated class and enjoying the detective work, I have to be grateful to Mr E (or Monsieur Teste, Valery's hyper-intellect as I am bound to think of him). But there are problems with the 'non-building'. The chief one is the perennial question with all Eisenman's work and most Neo-Modernism: who can decode it except for the author and his phalanx of expositors? This work is elitist, subjective (in spite of objectivist production) and, most damaging for Eisenman's latest position, 'repressive'. It represses not only traditional art in frames, but the experience of anyone who doesn't know what the 96-foot grid means, or can't perceive the pedantic difference between 'simulation' and 'dissimulation'.

If one looks through the random, but representative, list of the ten propositions, one can see that probably only numbers 4 and 7 are somewhat accessible. The public – students, Columbus citizens and art lovers – might perceive the non-building merging into its

environment and the white grid as a sign of scaffolding and therefore of an unfinished building. Also they might perceive the shifted grids as town versus campus. And indeed the hanging column is a very perceivable indicator of its non-structural role and the fractured brick curves are very, very perceivable signs of the old armoury. But the rest of the references – to the Greenville Line, and White Tower, and 30 or 40 subtleties of meaning – will probably be lost.

Take the 96-foot ordering grid, the white spine which sits over the top of the other grids and sends out perpendicular box beams every 96 feet. From within the main office one can see this light blank box coming to a sharp point – sliced off by the 12-foot white scaffold-grid. One might think it has some function – mechanical or otherwise – but it turns out to be an architectural ordering device, a 'not-cornice'. Eisenman mordantly calls it 'student housing' because of its minimalist appearance; but the public are as unlikely to understand this reference as its rhetorical role. Once one does perceive it as a 'not-cornice' and 96-foot grid, that is as a conceptual device, it gains in stature. As we were looking at these beams I wondered why Eisenman didn't provide clues to their meanings around the site – models, legends, drawings and diagrams set into the pavement – so that the conceptual meanings would become more accessible. After all, even Bernard Tschumi provides something like this at the entrance to the Parc de la Villette. Architecture, at the end of the day, is a public art. But Mr E seems caught at the moment between two equal and conflicting desires: to make architecture comprehensible and obscure.

Obscurity also gets the upper hand on the west garden side where the 'Greenville Trace' slices its way through the blank volumes and a representation of the flat Ohio prairie. On one level this will be a welcome background space, a space for sculpture, quiet contemplation and absent meaning. Three block volumes – which contain such things as the Black Box auditorium and recording studios – are surmounted by that 96-foot bland 'not-cornice'. Red stone walls tilt against each other continuing the Greenville slice – but who could possibly decode this referent? Perhaps some people appreciate that the blank masonry walls 'simulate' the pre-existing hall which has been chopped off, because it is literally joined by the same masonry; but the notional abstract detailing here is likely to suppress the awareness of architectural significance altogether.

I have three specific arguments with the abstractions here and in some other places. At a certain distance, about ten feet, the architecture looses interest, sensuality and detail. It becomes the 'built diagram' of Walter Gropius and Aldo Rossi, something more akin to cardboard than constructed architecture. It needs more of the 'self similarity' of scaling which the Gothic cathedral has and which Eisenman talks about – a transformation of patterns from 200 to two feet.

It also needs a greater ratio of figure to ground, representation to abstraction, convention to invention than it now reveals on the east and west garden sides. The 'non-entrance' with its juxtaposition of recognizable and alien shapes does have an effective ratio which holds the interest, whereas these back gardens feel like disregarded spaces, backgrounds in search of foreground figures. One feels that here the architect has lost his characteristic desire to represent a conundrum.

Indeed here we also come to the main problematic of Eisen-architecture. It suggests, like programme music, another text and, like the symbolic architecture of Egypt, an esoteric reading. Most forms and articulations have a precise, if arcane, referent and if one knows this it can stimulate a very enjoyable game of 'hunt the cryptic symbol'. The only drawback to this pleasure is that Eisenman keeps most of the codes to himself and they refer to relatively banal meanings – such as shifted grids, 'dissimulation' and the Greenville Trace. The Egyptians, after all, symbolised more significant matters – everyday life, the flooding of the Nile and the ordered cosmos – not an old armory or grid which happened to exist 100 years before.

Eisenman could answer that the client and the Art Centre as a building-type do not today allow more significant issues to be represented. We live in a fragmented, anonymous, de-humanized, boring, insignificant and agnostic universe and, if we are candid, must represent these truths. Something a bit like this, buttressed with Deconstructionist argument, and a nihilist metaphysics, might be his reply.

Modern and Neo-Modern Metaphysics
One of the great virtues of Eisenman, as of Le Corbusier before him, is his indefatigable attempt to symbolise the dominant views of science and the human condition without recourse to consoling philosophies that are wishful thinking, or accommodating half-truths.

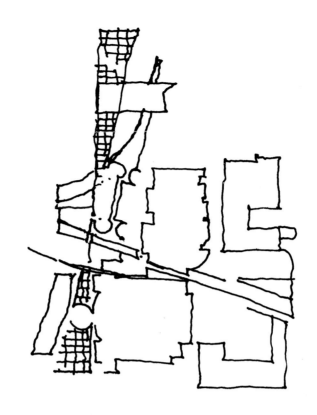

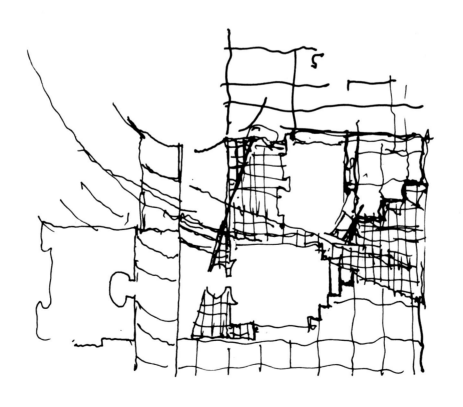

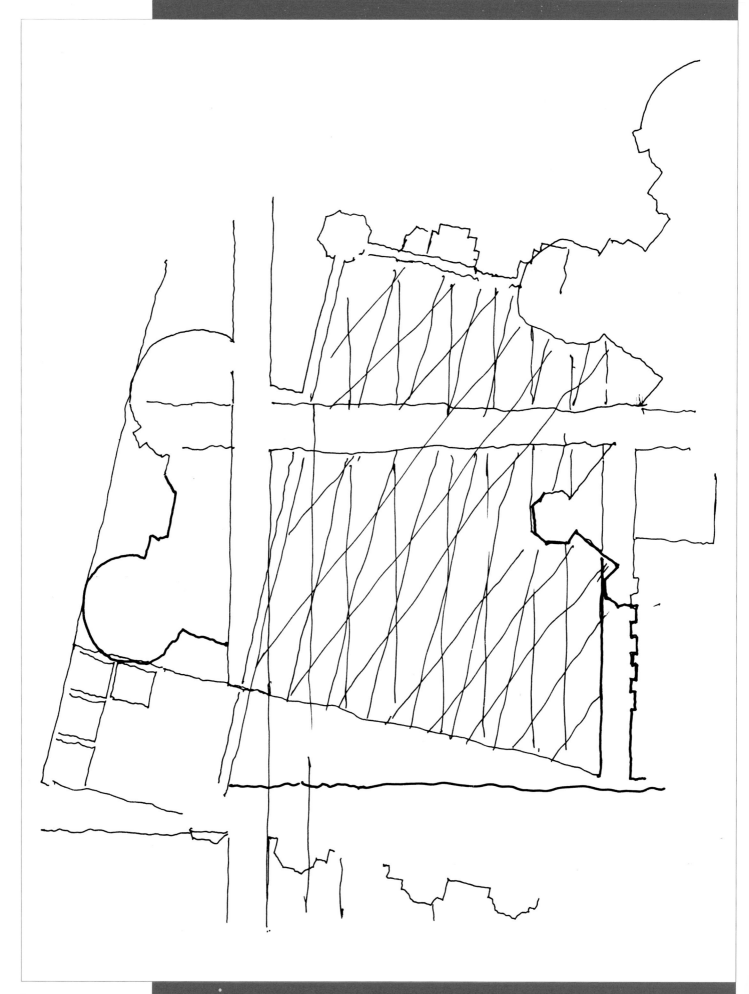

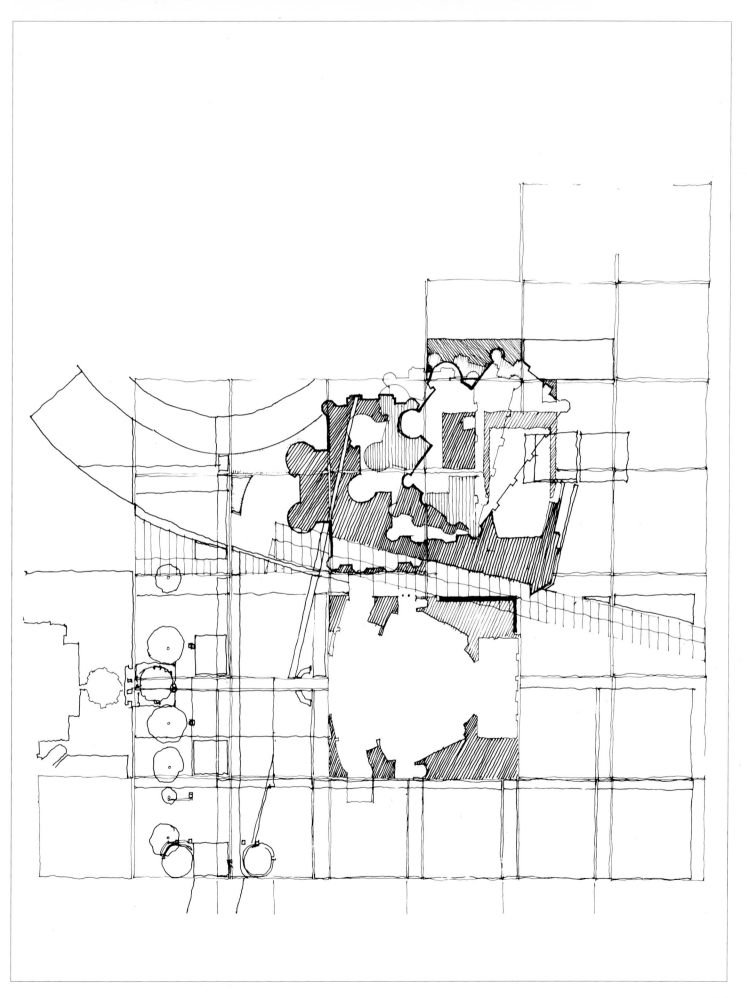

BETWEEN THE SPHERE AND THE LABYRINTH

R.E. SOMOL

Madness, you are no longer the object of the ambiguous praise with which the sage decorated the impregnable burrow of his fear; and if after all he finds himself tolerably at home there, it is only because the supreme agent forever at work digging its tunnels is none other than reason the very Logos that he serves. Jacques Lacan
Eisenman offers his 'meditations of Icarus', which know of the failures suffered during the 'diggings of the old mole'. Manfredo Tafuri

Peter Eisenman has completed the construction of his burrow and it seems to be successful. The Wexner Center for the Visual Arts a centre for the production and exhibition of experimental works in various media, combines Eisenman's early interest in formal autonomy with the processes of excavation and digging later explored in his Cannaregio project for Venice and House Eleven a. At Wexner, Eisenman exchanges and reassembles collective and personal narratives, collapsing references to an archaeology of the avant garde in America (ie, to the Armory Show of 1913) with a catalogue of his own strategies over the last 20 years. The skeletal extension of Wexner operates as *passe-partout* that opens a multiplicity of entrances and exits and frames a host of possible approaches and departures.

As in the Cannaregio, the figures of the museum and the house – the privileged public and private programmes of the modern canon – begin to infect one another at Wexner as movement and individual become indistinct. In its siting the structure materialises the urban element, the 'missing' central cruciform, of House X while inside it exploits and explodes the notational system of virtual, real and suspended columns employed in the earlier house schemes. This permanent installation, Eisenman's Armory Show, represents the most complete realisation yet of a practice that displaces the humanism and functionalism contained in both classical and modern architecture. Wexner achieves this not through its particular formal or figurative elements, but by experimenting with conditions of between and processes of becoming. These processes dominate all aspects of the project, including its objective, experiential and contextual conditions.

The initial archeological excavations at Ohio State provide the impetus for reconstructing fragments of the armory that had previously occupied part of the site. Here, Eisenman's burrowing emerges precisely as a form of castling and, as in the writings of Kafka, the castle and burrow become emblems for the multiple passageways and connections of the labyrinth. More specifically, the relationship of tower and grid at Wexner suggests a connection to castling in chess, the only move where two pieces are simultaneously in motion passing through one another and reversing positions. While Manfredo Tafuri has identified the contemporary vanguards as the 'new knights of purity', the hybridising process implicit in castling indicates a shift in orientation from the strategy of estrangement practiced by the historical avant garde.

For Viktor Shklovsky the poetic language of the avant garde was comparable to the 'knight's move'. As interpreted by Tafuri, this meant that 'like the discontinuous, L-shaped move of the "knight" in the game of chess, the semantic structure of the artistic product executes a "swerve", a side step, with respect to the real, thereby setting in motion a process of "estrangement" (Bertolt Brecht understood this well) and organising itself as a perpetual "surreality"'.[1] Certainly, Eisenman's house series sets up conditions of estrangement, and his later el-shaped structures hear a striking resemblance to the knight designed by Josef Hartwig for his 1924 chess set. Estrangement however, implies an encounter where subjects and objects confront one another, but remain essentially integral. The most interesting experiments of the neo-avant garde do not occur on the plane of the surreal, however, but in the process where hyperreal and hyperformal become indistinct. At Wexner, the sovereign grid (reason) is allowed a doubling two-step with the rook, its emissary and embodiment, suspending the laws of normal movement and development. This process proposes a third term for the avant garde object, between the sphere and the labyrinth, where the becoming-grid of the castle and the becoming-castle of the grid produce an imperceptibility. Ever since his opening move with House 1 (originally a white museum-pavilion for toys with its dominant figure of the man on horseback) Eisenman has been engaged in a game that desires the end of the practice that authorises its continuation. The castling move of Wexner is the most successful gambit yet in that the 'final structure exists in a state of between, a non-architectural supplement to architecture, part landscape and part scaffolding'.

This mutational design logic indicates that it would be unproductive to isolate or fixate on any particular figure (or author) in the Eisenman/Trott assemblage. Undoubtedly, some critics will focus exclusively on the fragmented armory forms located in the southwest corner of the site, drawing parallels to the work of James Wines, James Stirling or Michael Graves. Rather than serving as an example of Peter Eisenman's belated adoption of a figurative or historicist postmodernism, however, Wexner will more likely enable us to redefine what postmodernism was all along, to recover the contestatory aspects within postmodernism and undermine the facile stylistic history that has been marketed for the last decade. In other words, to overvalue either the figure of the skeletal frame or the ruined castle, to celebrate or condemn the project on the basis of either singular form, would be a mistake since in fact these two elements point toward each other and cannot be separated. Eisenman's comments on the work of Aldo Rossi are instructive for his own production which 'is an attempt to build a different kind of castle from that of the moderns. It is an elaborate scaffold erected for and by someone who can no longer climb its steps to die a hero's death'.[2] Wexner registers this transformational identity of the scaffold and the castle.

In addition to the process of excavation, the formal solution at Ohio State also results from the dynamic twisting and multiplication of two grids, those of the city and the campus, $12\frac{1}{2}$ degrees askew. In Wexner, Eisenman advances the grid to its conceptual and lyrical limits. Walking through the escalating layers of grids in the interior gallery or exterior arcade one begins to imagine the unimaginable: that somewhere on a rural Ohio farm there is a piece of the Wexner grid, even if registered only through an 'absent', fallow square. The limitation of the grid at Wexner, however, is that it can only induce a molar sublime, that it only works at the level of increasing magnification. The gridding process cannot be successfully reversed or miniaturised, for then the grid becomes a merely decorative and immobile thing, a fixture, as in the smallest grids at Wexner used to cover one set of the fluorescent lighting tubes.

In this way, the grid points out the need for a molecular sublime and confesses its own inability to *figuratively* provide that experience. Essentially, this raises the issue of whether the sublime can only be approached through the colossal, that which is too large for and overspills representation. In his discussion with Christopher Alexander, Eisenman indicates that he is interested in another sublime when he suggests that 'the too-small might also satisfy a feeling as well as the too-large.' Given the results at Wexner, however, the grid by itself seems an unlikely candidate to satisfy this need for a molecular sublime. In any case, there is a critical danger in developing a freeze-frame of either the castle or the grid. This observation – announced by the 'thing itself' at its (apparently) least successful moment – indicates that no strictly formal analysis of the object, the Wexner Center, is adequate to it, and that its real power can only be apprehended by engaging the situations it creates for observer and context. Wexner is most successful when it disappears, when it erases all planes of figure and ground, when its visibility is reduced to zero-zero.

Eisenman's practical, theoretical and historical investigations have always revolved around the displacement of the ground plane, man's upright datum, by floating or submerging it, by raising it and razing it, outbidding the terrestrial logic of an erect subjectivity. In Eisenman's projects, and particularly at Ohio State, the places of habitation are extraterrestrial and subterranean. Confronted with the prospect of being buried alive or placed in suspended animation, the inhabitant-user must abandon classical means for understanding the object as well as any self-satisfied liberal 'truths' about the post-Enlightenment subject. The mutual dependence of subject and object, their dissolution in a network of multiplicities, engenders the necessity for a becoming-bird or a becoming-mole. As in the inversion of king and rook (reason and desire) implicit in the object-process of castling, Wexner again raises the ambiguity of who or what is sovereign at the level of experience.

This attempt to estrange and activate the viewer is especially appropriate for an institution that promotes the production and display of art. The Wexner Center thus operates to challenge the institution and the works that it simultaneously protects and frames. The procedural scheme of Wexner suggests that the project of looking and evaluating cannot be conducted from an innocently distant and contemplative space, but that the eye is always in a body (even one that is constantly evolving) and that the building must therefore recognise and exhibit tactile and theatrical conditions of reception for itself as well as for the objects it houses. In Wexner, the triadic relationship among viewer, object and setting is made thematic with each term sliding into and redefining the others. If there is one consistent strategy manifested throughout the project it consists in this dissipation of hardened boundaries and established contexts and codes.

Even a cursory glance at the Wexner site plan indicates that the abaxial open grid forms a diagonal slash between Mershon Auditorium and Wiegel Hall. This aerial notation suggests that the project situates itself on (and as) the virgule, the solidus. As Jeffrey Kipnis has remarked of the Eisenman-Derrida collaboration at La Villette, Wexner, too, engages in 'twisting the separatrix', and attempts to destabilise traditional hierarchies and oppositions. As noted earlier, not the least among these in liberal political thought is the one separating private and public or, as expressed in modern architecture, the house and the museum. In fact, Wexner participates in a curious architectural line of thought that investigates – alternatively promoting, contesting, or merely marking – the contemporary experience of the domestication of the museum and the museumification of the domestic, the safe intimacy of stockpiled cultural objects and the mass mediated recording and exhibition of private life.

47

In his April 1, 1974 Postscript to *Five Architects* Philip Johnson wondered of Eisenman, 'What would he do in a large building?' Eisenman's response, most fully articulated in the Wexner Center, revolves around a reconsideration of Johnson's own Glass House. In his 1979 Introduction to Johnson's *Writings*, Eisenman concludes by focusing on a 'casual text caption' written by Johnson in 1950 to describe one of his primary design sources. Eisenman reproduces the caption in full, except for the last two sentences (here italicised):

The cylinder, made of the same brick as the platform from which it springs, forming the main *motif* of the house, was not derived from Mies, but rather from a burnt wooden village I saw once where nothing was left but foundations and chimneys of brick. *Over the chimney I slipped a steel cage with a glass skin. The chimney forms the anchor.*[4]

For Eisenman, the Glass House represents Johnson's 'monument to the horrors of war', an architectural object peculiarly situated to register the implications of the historic rupture of 1945. Significantly, one of the many questions this house answers is that posed by Johnson of Eisenman.[5] In the Ohio State project, one of his largest completed public structures, Eisenman blows up Johnson's domestic ruin, slipping a steel cage over the brick ruin of a cylindrical Armory tower.

Historically, perhaps the 'missing link' in the trajectory from the Glass House to the Wexner Center is, improbable as it may seem, Robert Venturi's Franklin Court, a garden-house-museum from 1972. Venturi's miniature, discrete urban complex consists of open, white steel frame 'ghost structures' – the arrangement of which establishes an extreme perspectival directionality to generate movement and passage – floated above brick foundations and subterranean ruins. In addition to exploring and eroding the house/museum (private/public) dichotomy, Venturi's Philadelphia experiment initiates the disappearance of architecture in favor of landscape (here, a slightly overscaled, eighteenth-century garden), archeological excavation and framing. At Franklin Court, as at Wexner, architecture begins its underground exile, an exile already charted at Johnson's New Caanen estate with his underground painting gallery (1966). Like Johnson's postwar residence, the fact that the ghost structures of Franklin Court appear precisely on the edge of a historical moment enables them to beautifully figure, but not yet respond to, this implicit transformation from arbor to burrow, from bower to bowels. It is this challenge of developing a post-arboreal architecture that Eisenman pursues at Ohio State.

The Wexner Center for the Visual Arts appears to be of uncertain size and indeterminate end largely due to its most literal between condition, serving as a suture for Mershon Auditorium and Weigel Hall. As a weed that proliferates within the spaces left between cultivated areas, between the institutions of cultural modernism and the structures of architectural modernity, Wexner approaches the status of a rhizome – a horizontal underground stem able to produce the shoot and root systems of a new plant. For the philosopher Gilles Deleuze, rhizomes include bulbs and tubers, animals in their pack form, weeds, and even burrows 'in all of their functions of shelter, supply, movement, elation and breakout'.[6] Deleuze's description of the rhizome – in contrast to the tree or root – can serve equally well as an account of Wexner:

A rhizome may be broken, shattered at a given spot, but it will start up again on one of its old lines, or on new lines ... [U]nlike trees or their roots, the rhizome connects any point to any other point, and its traits are not necessarily linked to traits of the same nature; it brings into play very different regimes of signs, and even nonsign states ... It is composed not of units but of dimensions, or rather directions in motion. It has neither beginning nor end, but always a middle from which it grows and which it overspills. It constitutes linear multiplicities with *n* dimensions having neither subject nor object.[7]

Inside and out, Wexner is constructed as a series of plateaus without origin or finality. Particularly within the inversely pitched gallery and arcade passages of the central circulation spine that set up exaggerated perspectival vanishing points, Wexner establishes converging lines of flight and mobility that destratify the site and programme.

In contrast to the vertical or hierarchical model of the tree and root which would require an evaluative criterion of formal competence and entail a contemplative experience (ie, the building as accurate tracing from a proper model), Wexner fabricates a lateral mapping of the site that can only be understood through a criterion of performance and a tactile reception strategy. This rhizomatic aspect marks the project's greatest contribution to a critical architecture distinct from the Classical-enlightenment tradition and opposed to contemporary practices that masquerade as the progeny of that lineage. This proposal for an avant garde architectural practice is perhaps most fully delineated in the four quadrants constituted through the Wexner intervention.

As mock historical narrative, the first three quadrants (southeast, southwest and northwest) refer to architectural types from the mid-eighteenth, -nineteenth, and -twentieth centuries respectively: the formal garden of the rationally gridded buckeye trees, the solid masonry of the reconstructed armory, and the banal late-modern box continued from the side wall elevation of Weigel Hall. From this perspective, Eisenman's alternative paradigm is most readily displayed in the northeast quadrant where a maze of landscaping – one that rises above street level yet none the less induces the experience of being underground and below variously inclining embankments of earth and weeds – becomes aligned with the intersecting strands of unevenly pitched grids that form Wexner's central spine. This implied equivalence between weed and architecture does not result from resemblance or imitation, but from an aparallel evolution, distinct from the continuous tripartite history simulated in the first three quadrants.

Within the northeast corner of the Ohio State site, then, a line of escape, of becoming and imperceptibility, can be recognised. Only nascent in the Wexner scheme, this architectural organisation has become increasingly evident in some of the more recent projects coming out of Eisenman's office, projects that largely abandon the grid altogether. In this way, the tubular strands that are being referred to as 'worms' in the proposals for the Columbus Convention Center and the Barcelona hotel might more accurately be described as rhizomes. The most promising of the new designs may be the one for the College of Design, Art, Architecture and Planning at the University of Cincinnati where curved and oscillating line segments are embedded in a basically rectilinear modern structure, proliferating opportunities for mutational exchange. This new orientation represents a break with the architectural discipline instituted under the Enlightenment with Laugier's model of the primitive hut, an undermining of the domestic tree metaphor that has petrified architectural discourse for a least the last two centuries.

Wexner is not an arborescent architecture, not a tree house; it is not involved with roots, origins or ends. As Deleuze and Guattari write of the rhizome, it 'is not the object of reproduction: neither external reproduction as image-tree nor internal reproduction as tree-structure'.[8] In this, Wexner operates in marked contrast to what may be the last great arboreal architectural work in America, Frank Lloyd Wright's Johnson Wax complex, which combines a symbolic representation of the primative hut with its dendriform columns and cantilevered Research Tower with a structural system based on a homology with the taproot. Wexner represents the most fully articulated postwar alternative to Wright's hierarchically organised, differentiated, unidirectional and anti-urban model from which the profession developed a peculiarly American modernism. It is precisely this reconstruction of modernism in postwar America, with its concommitant institutionalisation of the profession, that propelled the discipline into a crisis beginning in the mid-60s and that generated the recovery of certain techniques and practices of the historical European avant garde.

Unlike the tree that imposes a hierarchical or pyramidal structure and that establishes a vertical discourse of power, the rhizome circulates underground making unordered connections and affiliations, sometimes penetrating even the rooted trunks of trees and putting them to new uses. 'A method of the rhizome type', Deleuze and Guattari declare, 'can analyze language only be decentring it on to other dimensions and other registers.'[9] At Ohio State this critical-parasitic procedure can be apprehended most readily in the 'Greenville Trace' that cuts through the landscape and structure at the northern end of the site, shifting and shearing what otherwise would have been the 'routine' collision of the city and campus grids. Originally, the Ohio territory was plotted by two teams of surveyors whose grids were supposed to meet on an east-west axis that runs through Columbus. Since the calculations were off, however, the teams missed this linear connection, the Greenville line, and the grids failed to connect. The Wexner Center allows this history to be recovered, a history that the politics of mapping and the discipline of cartography had to supress, by registering the missed connection through a hybrid formal condition. Wexner demonstrates that even missed or hidden connections leave their mark. It establishes a non-binary, non-totalising multiplicity of n-1 dimensions.

Strictly speaking, the Wexner Center has no identity, and the entire critical endeavour of trying to establish one may be misguided from the beginning. With Wexner, Peter Eisenman instigates a 'para-architecture', one which pushes reason to unreasonable speculation, inventing histories and deploying coincidences to escape tradition. These multiplications of entryways and fictions, however, exhibit an incredible specificity with regard to the site and programme at Ohio State. While the deterritorialising process undertaken at Wexner raises the possibility for a critical architecture and a regionalism without roots, it is not a formal model to be copied or imitated.

As new as it is, the nearly completed Wexner Center for the Visual Arts already represents a transitional project in Eisenman's production, an inevitably between-work. As the last project to employ the grid as a dominant formal and structural motif it has connections to the earliest house schemes that attempted to uncover the deep structure of architecture. In its deployment of processes of becoming and techniques of mapping Wexner is also the first in a series of post-arboreal, rhizomatic entities currently in various stages of design and construction. Ultimately, however, the potential for developing a molecular architecture may require rethinking or refining Eisenman's historiography. The rupture of 1945 may no longer be the most powerful postwar break, and conclusions founded solely on its implications may occlude others. As suggested in the discussion of Franklin Court, a more recent transition – eg, between the late-sixties and early-seventies – requires an alternative cultural-political tactic. The major obstacle to mutable and recombinant personal and collective relations today are miniaturised and internal: bugs, not bombs; deterrence, not destruction. The burrows of postmodernism should not be mistaken for nuclear shelters. The post-1972 cultural formation is dominated not by the threat of extinction but by the networks of surveillance, security, and testing that are ostensibly maintained to prevent it.

The success of the Wexner Center is that it challenges the institutions and discourses, including but not limited to those of the performing and visual arts, developed to ensure boundary maintenance and a proper, natural order. The threat, of course, is from the same power discourses that will reconstruct an object, reterritorialise the project, turning this text into a unique work, an object of contemplation. In the end, only a performative piece of advice can be offered, a futurist footnote. The Wexner Center, Peter

Eisenman's response to Philip's April Fool's Day question, is a map to be extended and an object to be destroyed, demanding enlargement and tempting annihilation: blow it up.

Notes
1 Manfredo Tafuri, *The Sphere and the Labyrinth*, MIT Press, Cambridge MA, 1987, p 16.
.2 Peter Eisenman, 'The Houses of Memory: The Texts of Analogy', Introduction to *The Architecture of the City*, by Aldo Rossi, MIT Press, Cambridge MA, 1982, p 4.
3 'Contrasting Concepts of Harmony in Architecture', *Lotus International* 40, 1983, p 65.
4 Philip Johnson, 'House at New Canaan, Connecticut', from *Writings* Oxford University Press, New York, 1979, p 223. Also, see Eisenman's Introduction, pp 23-3.
5 As Eisenman writes, 'I know of no other house that answers so many questions . . . ' *Id*, p 23.
6 Gilles Deleuze and Felix Guatari, *A Thousand Plateaus*, trans by Brian Massumi, University of Minnesota Press, Minneapolis MN, 1987, pp 6-7.
7 *Id*, pp 8 and 21.
8 Deleuze and Guattari, p 22.
9 *Id*, p 8.

A FRAMEWORK FOR THE FUTURE

KURT W. FORSTER

Visitors to a new building, even when they come prepared, do well to avoid 'formal' introductions – that is, main entrances – an instead to spirit their way in through the proverbial 'back door'. To be sure, surreptitious entry into a public or private building can ge one into trouble, and typically leaves one disoriented; nevertheless, in the instance of Peter Eisenman's Wexner Center[1] on the campu of Ohio State University, Columbus, the 'back-door' approach may well be the best choice, the one most in keeping with the actu nature of the building. Armed with note pad and camera, I sneaked into the well-guarded construction site, followed a corridor, an scaled a ladder leading up to the rooftop, only to discover that on the roof, I remained almost as much 'inside' the building – an certainly inside its peculiar framework – as I had been kept 'outside' while I wandered through its interior corridors and passageway A less furtive approach than mine, or even casual daily use in the future, is likely to reveal similar contradictions in the very terms c architectural experience. Visitors are repeatedly asked to overstep, invert, suspend, or embrace such contradictions as they follow th many and varied passages within, about, and through the building.

The Wexner Center represents the first complete realisation of Eisenman's architecture in the United States, and it makes a powerf counter-statement to the current crop of massive cultural institutions which have begun to rear their blind heads from Washingto D.C. to Dallas to Orange County. These projects tend to result in monoliths whose volumes have all the subtlety of a giant wedge c cheese, and whose urban presence depends on a *cordon sanitaire* of irrigated lawn and vacant granite plazas. But there are signs c other approaches: Richard Meier's master plan for the new Getty Center in Brentwood, Frank Gehry's Disney Concert Hall in Lc Angeles[2] – if the project can be realised as Gehry originally conceived it – and now, for all to see, Eisenman's Wexner Center. Howeve remote Eisenman's work may stand from either of these other two examples, it shares ideas with Gehry's recent thinking about th place of the 'new' within its context, and about the capabilities of architectural imagination. In sharp contrast to the encroachir extremes of programmatic determination, Gehry and Eisenman bring programmatic flexibility into a rapport with architectur ndeterminacy. In obvious ways, both of them let certain architectural events occur at the same time as they allow for elements that ar not of the same origin as the design itself.

To begin with, the physical extent of Eisenman's Wexner Center is deliberately blurred and its limits erased to the point c dissimulation. In a few years, who will suspect Eisenman's handiwork in a diagonally-scored sidewalk, in a grove of buckeye and gink rees, or in strangely canted planting beds? In time, it will appear as if the architect had merely strung together parts and pieces of th surrounding buildings and spaces – whose materials both echo and contrast with one another – and resurrected small fragments of th huge Armory that once occupied this quadrant of the campus. These fragments, faced with brick and unsentimentally cut apart or sur below ground, resemble giant chess pieces set against the conventional scale of surrounding buildings. Is it far-fetched to suggest tha this is precisely how historic architecture appears today, and how its sudden, fragmentary, and often scale-less reappearance makes fc the disconcerting effect of much postmodern architecture?

n Eisenman's case, the difference lies not only in the cunning way in which he estranges the familiar, but also in the fact that he returr to an episode from the history of the site that has been 'invisible' for 30 years. When Eisenman renders a part of his architecture figura he often reveals something invisible: here, it is the fragments of a now-destroyed campus landmark; in the Frankfurt project for th Biology Center of the University[3], it was a volumetric analogy to the configuration of molecular elements in the gene structure. By suc acts of arbitrary choice and in his deliberate promotion of such elements to the status of building parts, Eisenman engineers a built-i conflict, a figural counterpoint to those elements which belong to the client's programme or result from the architect's own prompting What do these external elements convey, especially when they are caught within a system of abstract scaffolds, a cage of lines incise nto the ground, scored on the windows and ceilings, and set up virtually throughout the buildings as a framework of posts and beam assuming no obvious structural burden? Eisenman stages the counterpoint between elements of a resistant reality – be they of a figura or programmatic character – and an order of his own invention. Not that the component parts of this invention are very original, nc he fragments of external origin necessarily 'found', but this counterplay between 'borrowed' and 'found' parts, between insisten geometric abstraction and curiously orphaned fragments of reality, reaches a compelling manifestation in the Wexner Center.

the series of Eisenman Houses tried to expunge the personal by means of a generative geometric process endowed with its own logic, he projects for Berlin (Kochstrasse), Columbus, Ohio, and Frankfurt each adopt extraneous elements which resist the architect's will y definition. To be sure, Eisenman has made it appear that way even where he was clearly free to do otherwise, but what matters more is the role these elements are given to play in his architecture. This role is one of resistance to the architect's liberty, but as soon s these fragments of existing architecture manifest their unyielding presence, they proffer themselves as shapes, as parts that are lready designed and therefore predate the workings of Eisenman's mind. Whether he intends them to exercise their power or not, hey condition his work by withstanding its drive for totality and autonomy. They substitute for otherwise absent historical conditions nd resist the purely internal resolution of any architectural parti. History recedes into the ground like cracks that break the soil after he water has long since evaporated. Alan Colquhoun has characterised the Ohio project 'as purely interstitial, avoiding the problem of acades,'[4] and, indeed, what there are of 'facades' belong either to the category of borrowed elements or to that of mere screens. The creens hide nothing, and the found elements are remade. As a result, the resistance Eisenman prefigures into his projects is the mere ppearance of resistence. Such fictional reality, like a mystery guest, leaves behind a garment of unfamiliar cloth whose pattern and abric are suddenly those of a mere shroud.

isenman deploys these figments of reality like actual fragments and inscribes his own conditions into the design by rendering them oddly 'interstitial'. In a word, the resistance of reality turns into fiction, and Eisenman's fiction into the singular reality of the project. uch an inversion of terms is not brought about by an act of sophistry, but rather by design, design capable of setting its own terms. isenman engineers the counterplay between external demands and internal imperatives as the inner spring of his invention. How such process works in actual instance the Wexner Center can now demonstrate. Where the Berlin building on the Kochstrasse fell short largely due to a severely truncated execution – and what the project for the California State University at Long Beach could not put o the test, the Wexner Center for the Visual Arts presents to us in a full and authentic realization.

isenman's architecture proves itself capable of an appropriately contradictory result: it is both extensive and penetrating, and at the ame time removed, not to say suspended, from its site. This it accomplishes by means of a multiple system of referents, both physically vithin view from one or another of its prospects, and subliminally perceived on virtually every surface of the Structure. Two ntersecting passageways frame the visitor's approach like trellises, and, even while one remains 'outside', cast their perspectives across he site. Large volumes rise from the surrounding ground – beautifully faced in red sandstone and variously canted – vaguely suggesting relationship between their half-hidden shapes and the surrounding buildings whose external walls are revetted with precisely the ame materials.

hese external Cross-passages find their counterparts on the inside, where two principal scaffoldings – differently dimensioned, but otherwise indistinguishable – intersect and, occasionally, interpenetrate. The moments of their intersection, and the corresponding novement of volumes, produce a spatial polyphony of breathtaking order, accentuated by a virtually orchestral density of markings, ubtle differentiation, and a new kind of encoding of every surface. Stone pavement and wood flooring patterns, mullions, tinted vindow glass, layered walls and ceilings all rush into concordance with this polyphony, a polyphony that sets its cadences with volumes nd posts, and scales everything to its vistas. This composite order rests on the integration of innumerable elements, many among them tock supplies: Eisenman has arrayed even fluorescent tubes of standard lengths to articulate, by their location and alignment, the larger patial order of the entire structure. Simple wire cages that house them participate, as do many other 'purely' utilitarian elements, in an lmost overwhelmingly complete exposition of the building's architectural premises.

he main internal gallery, running the length of the building between the external corridor to one side and the expanding volumes of xhibition spaces on the other, finds its accompaniment in a narrow diagonal passageway ascending from level to level over flights of tairs, finally terminating in a spy window. According to a typical strategy, Eisenman opens the exhibition spaces laterally off the long allery and divides them, if at all, with sliding doors, while he dramatizes the entrance and descent into the building with the curvature of the Armory towers and sharp turn of the stairs – over which a vacant scaffold rises as a counter-theme – as well as with the signature hanging' column.

he most remarkable thing about the Wexner Center is its eminently architectural qualities. This will seem a strange commentary on building *only* if one forgets the familiar critique of Eisenman's architecture: that it is abstract, willful, and best built of cardboard. nstead, the early, sometimes tortuous, complexities of his designs have yielded here to great clarity of exposition and mature reatment of all aspects of execution. This is an architecture of density and coherence in all its tightly-related parts, one which denies othing of its physical reality, and which extends, in presence and impact, far beyond the limited compass of its site. The landscapes of tone-faced volumes on both of its rear sides (toward West Seventeenth Avenue) possess as much poetry as do the building's most visible aspects. And, the rapidly changing echo of one's footfall moving along the interior passageways lends yet another *physical* dimension to their abstract presence.

The twin scaffoldings , exposed in their emptiness on the outside while intersecting with volumes on the inside, recall the grids erected by El Lissitzky for 'Film und Foto: International Exhibition of the Werkbund', at Stuttgart in 1929 , and adopted by Edoardo Persico and Marcello Nizzoli in a publicity construction designed for the Plebescite and installed in Milan's huge Galleria Vittorio Emanuele in 1934, not to mention Giuseppe Terragni's use of the partially exposed inner grid in the posts and beams of his Casa del Fascio in Como, 1932-1936. These stand as key instances where the necessarily abstract order of architectural means is counterposed with the bits and pieces of reality as they are typically presented in photographs, those archetypal fragments of modern reality. Eisenman's design recalls these instances of contrapuntal order, but it is not inspired by nostalgia or historicism.

Only within a framework can historic fragments exercise their poetic resistance, only within a scaffolding of reference can contemporary uses acquire their edge and future purpose. That these relationships are always imbalanced and continuously in need of reflection constitutes the truth of any rapport with the past. Both in their physical reality and as metaphor, Roman monuments encased in neatly constructed modern scaffoldings for their protection during cleaning and restoration make a provocative comparison with Eisenman's deliberate exposition of (made) historic remnants on existing ground and in a pre-existing context — both highly charged — through the perspective device of his abstract architectural order .

Notes
1 At the time of the competition in 1983, the exact designation of the architectural consortium was Eisenman/Robertson, and Trott & Bean. The subsequent development of the plans for construction was carried out by Eisenman, Architects, and Trott & Bean, Architects. For simplicity's sake, and because the project is discussed here chiefly in terms of its place within the evolution of Peter Eisenman's architectural thinking, the authorship has usually been abbreviated as 'Eisenman'. This slights in no way the substantial share that Trott & Bean, Architects have had in carrying this highly demanding complex from its conceptual beginnings into architectural reality.
2 See my 'The Snake and the Fish on the Hill', in *Zodiac* 2 (1989), 180-195.
3 See 'Peter Eisenman: Biology Center for the J.W. Goethe University of Frankfurt, Frankfurt-am-Main, 1987,' in *Assemblage* 5 (1988), 29-50.
4 In *A Center for the Visual Arts, the Ohio State University Competition*, ed. by Peter Arnell and Ted Bickford (New York: Rizzoli, 1984), 134; cf. my 'Traces and Treason of a Tradition: A Critical Commentary on Graves' and Eisenman/Robertson's Projects for the Ohio State University Center for the Visual Arts' in the same volume.

PETER EISENMAN FAIA

Peter Eisenman is an architect and educator. He was the founder and former Director of the Institute for Architecture and Urban Studies in New York City. He has designed a wide range of prototypical large-scale projects and a series of innovative private houses. Mr Eisenman is working on projects for Carnegie Mellon Research Institute, the University of Cincinnati College of Art, Architecture, Design, and Planning, an office building in Tokyo, social housing at the Hague, and the $43 million Wexner Center for the Visual Arts in Columbus, Ohio, a joint venture with Richard Trott. Mr Eisenman is a recipient of a Guggenheim Fellowship, the Brunner Award of the American Academy of Arts and Letters, and most recently, a grant from the National Endowment for the Arts. He has received several awards from Progressive Architecture and the AIA. He has taught at many colleges and universities, and is currently the first Irwin S Chanin Distinguished Professor of Architecture at the Cooper Union in New York City and the Louis Sullivan Professor of Architecture at the University of Illinois – Chicago. He was the Editor of Oppositions Journal and Opositions Books, and he is the author of several books, including *House X* (Rizzoli), *Fin d'Ou T HouS* and *Moving Arrows, Eros and Other Errors* (The Architectural Association).

RICHARD W TROTT FAIA

Richard Trott founded Richard Trott and Partners in 1965. Through his leadership the firm has been recognized with over 80 awards and was especially honoured in 1986 when they were named the first ever Ohio recipient of the 'Gold Medal' award from the American Institute of Architects as Ohio's outstanding firm. Active in many professional and civic affairs, Mr Trott also is an Adjunct Professor of Architecture at the Ohio State University.

Mr Trott has enjoyed particular success in designing corporate facilities and retail centers. His corporate headquarters design for Sherex (Shering AG, West Berlin) was selected as the top new research laboratory in the nation in 1982. The master plan for Milan Italy's U S A facilities for Adria and Erbamont/NV also received a national award in 1988. Other award winning facilities include ITT's, O M Scott which was published nationally by Whitney publication's *Corporate Design* and by the AIA's *Architecture* journal, Chemlawn Corporate Headquarters, Rax Systems Headquarters, and Farmers Insurance of Los Angeles operations centers in Columbus and Chicago.

His design for the Wexner Center for the Visual Arts, in partnership with Peter Eisenman, won an international competition.